Jim Henson's
THE DARK CRYSTAL
AGE OF RESISTANCE

DREAM-SEEKING

QUIZZES, TRIVIA, AND ADVENTURE

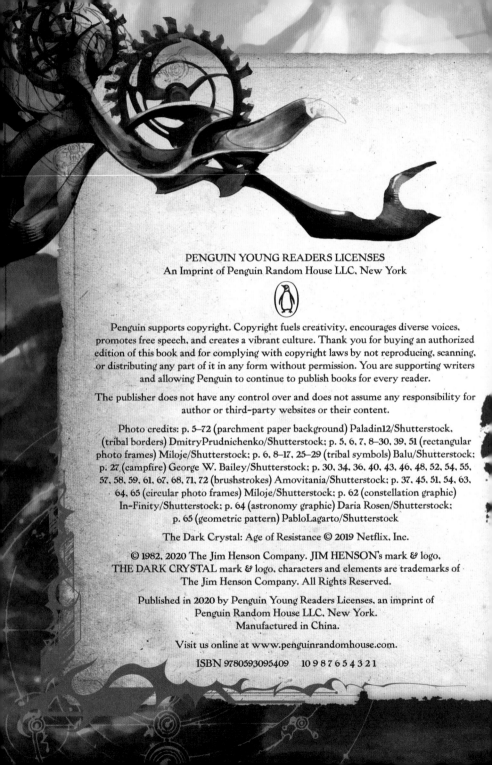

PENGUIN YOUNG READERS LICENSES
An Imprint of Penguin Random House LLC, New York

Photo credits: p. 5–72 (parchment paper background) Paladin12/Shutterstock, (tribal borders) DmitryPrudnichenko/Shutterstock; p. 5, 6, 7, 8–30, 39, 51 (rectangular photo frames) Miloje/Shutterstock; p. 6, 8–17, 25–29 (tribal symbols) Balu/Shutterstock; p. 27 (campfire) George W. Bailey/Shutterstock; p. 30, 34, 36, 40, 43, 46, 48, 52, 54, 55, 57, 58, 59, 61, 67, 68, 71, 72 (brushstrokes) Amovitania/Shutterstock; p. 37, 45, 51, 54, 63, 64, 65 (circular photo frames) Miloje/Shutterstock; p. 62 (constellation graphic) In-Finity/Shutterstock; p. 64 (astronomy graphic) Daria Rosen/Shutterstock; p. 65 (geometric pattern) PabloLagarto/Shutterstock

Published in 2020 by Penguin Young Readers Licenses, an imprint of Penguin Random House LLC, New York.
Manufactured in China.

Visit us online at www.penguinrandomhouse.com.

ISBN 9780593095409   10 9 8 7 6 5 4 3 2 1

Jim Henson's
THE DARK CRYSTAL
AGE OF RESISTANCE

DREAM-SEEKING

QUIZZES, TRIVIA, AND ADVENTURE

BY MILLER WALTON

TABLE OF CONTENTS

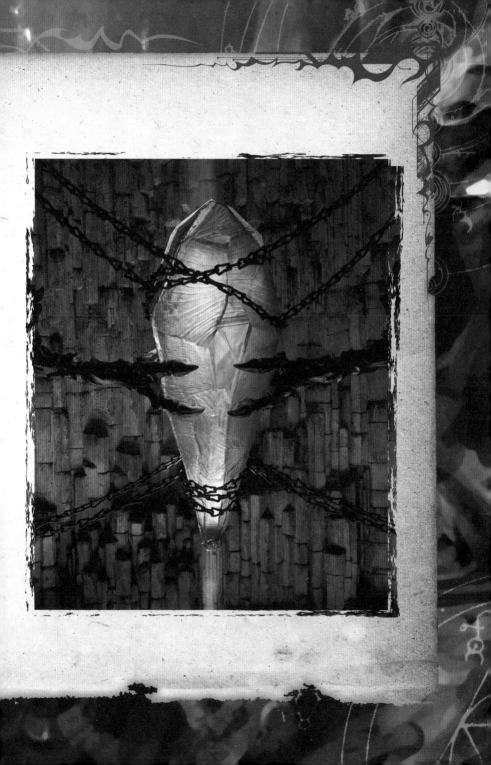

Find the Path to Your Gelfling Clan

You are a young Gelfling leaving home for the first time. You pack your meager belongings and say goodbye to your friends. As the three suns rise, you take your first steps out into the world beyond your village. You take in a deep breath of cool morning air and open your eyes to the wonders that wait ahead of you, ready to spread your wings and explore new places and meet new people. Maybe even find a new home and clan to call family.

To your left, a mountain range rises out of the dense green Endless Forest. The mountains are mysterious and majestic, the forest rife with adventure and life. Danger—like a growling Fizzgig—lurks in every hollow and cave, but so too does beauty.

To your right, the plains unfurl in gentle slopes. Somewhere beyond them are the Crystal Desert and the Silver Sea. Both are known to be dangerous places where only the most resourceful and intuitive Gelfling can survive.

WHICH WAY DO YOU GO?
TO GO TO THE MOUNTAINS AND THE WOODS, GO TO 1.
TO GO TO THE DESERT AND THE SEA, GO TO 2.

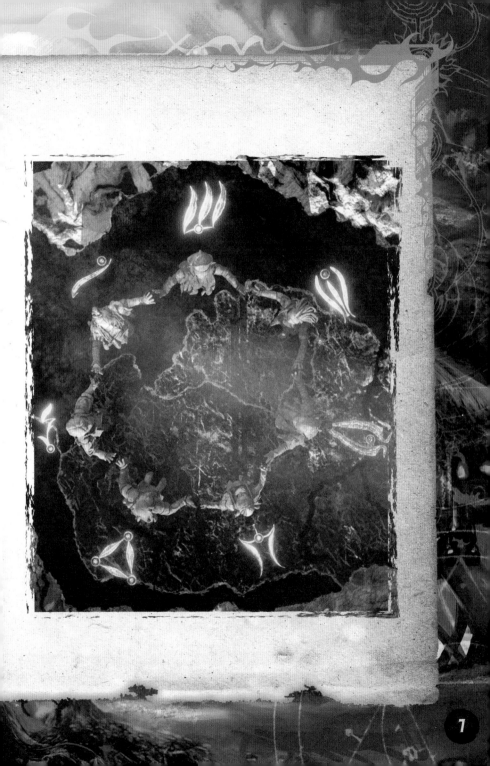

1. TO THE MOUNTAINS AND THE WOODS

With great determination, you head toward the woods. The mountain range borders the far tree line, dusty and gray. One mountain in particular seems to shine as the morning light glints off it. It looks like a beacon. A waypoint. With that peak always in sight, you will never lose your way.

You enter the woods. The lush scent of the trees surrounds you, damp and fresh, and hundreds of birds and other critters serenade you from the emerald canopy. A trail twists through the trees, over sparkling creeks and around boulders covered in dancing mushrooms. You follow the trail along a creek to a point where it splits.

One tail of the path cuts deeper into the Endless Forest. You've heard songs that say that somewhere deep within the forest is Stone-in-the-Wood, the home of the industrious Stonewood clan. There, you could share a hearth with other Gelfling and exchange songs of adventures.

The other path crosses the river and winds upward, into a higher, rocky terrain that will eventually become the mountains that border the wood. The caves and crevices within the steep cliffs are full of mystery and wonder, and of course to climb the mountains would be quite a feat. It may not be easy, but it would certainly be a chance to prove your fortitude—if not to others, then certainly to yourself.

WHICH PATH WILL YOU CHOOSE?
TO GO DEEPER INTO THE WOODS, GO TO 3.
TO GO INTO THE MOUNTAINS, GO TO 4.

2. TO THE DESERT AND THE SEA

The open sky calls to you, and so you answer, stepping into the soft plains covered in gently waving grasses and whistling wildflowers. There is no path or trail, but you don't need one; it's easy to find landmarks along the horizon, and the earth is soft and gentle beneath your feet. Before long, the wood and the mountains disappear behind you.

You walk for some time, until the grass is broken by patches of sparkling, crystalline soil. You stand at the edge of a vast shimmering sea of sand.

Far, far away, brushing the horizon of the crystal dunes, are the moons. They are nearly invisible, just milky dots of white in the sky. They seem to sing of an ocean just as endless as the desert . . .

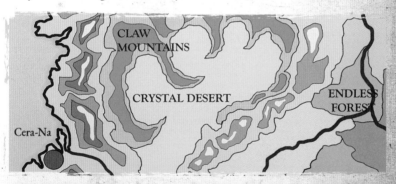

WHICH PATH WILL YOU CHOOSE?
TO GO INTO THE DESERT, GO TO 18.
TO FOLLOW THE MOONS TO THE SEA, GO TO 19.

3. GO DEEPER INTO THE WOODS

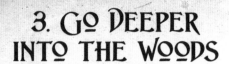

Eager for the chance to meet other Gelfling and explore the sprawling, tangled trees, you head deeper into the Endless Forest. Light dapples the loamy path with gold, and the soil all around smells rich and earthy. Furry critters scamper along the tree branches, long tails coiled in curly loops.

After a while, your trail intersects a deep ravine. Below you can see water moving at a quick pace, sparkling and ebony. A rope bridge crosses over the ravine, stretching to the other side, where your path continues. Beyond, you can see that the trail widens, marked on either side with carefully placed stones. You must be getting close to Stone-in-the-Wood!

But the bridge has seen better days. The rope is frayed in places, brittle and thin. It is possible it may not even hold your Gelfling weight. There is sure to be a way to continue on your journey, but perhaps it does not mean following the trail.

WHAT DO YOU DO?

TO TAKE THE BRIDGE AND CONTINUE ON THE TRAIL, GO TO 5.

TO FIND YOUR OWN WAY, GO TO 7.

4. HIKE INTO THE MOUNTAINS

The challenge of the mountains brings a burst of energy to your footsteps, your heart already pounding in anticipation. So on the hike you go, following the rocky steps and trails as they ascend steeply into the blue and gray cliffs. Trees cling to the boulders and grow up between narrow crevices, fed by the thin streams that wind through the rocks and trickle down in shimmering waterfalls. The climb is not easy, but when you reach a landing, the breathtaking view makes your effort worth it.

You behold the sprawling landscape below you, from the woods to the plains beyond, all framed by the distant golden desert and the suns in the blue sky above, and feel content. After a moment you continue on your way up the mountain path. As you do, do you find yourself . . .

. . . FOCUSED ON THE JOURNEY? GO TO 21.
. . . FOCUSED ON YOUR DESTINATION? GO TO 22.

5. Take the Bridge

You take hold of the bridge's hand rope and make your way across the bridge as quickly—yet as carefully—as you can. The planks swing wildly under your feet. You nearly lose your balance but make it to the other side just as the rope snaps! The bridge drops away into the ravine, but you've already arrived safely on the other side. You take a moment to catch your breath, then head down the clearly marked trail laid out before you.

The trail curves through the wood, marked by stones and the occasional spear decorated with brightly colored ribbon. The trees open off one side of the wide path, giving you a clear view of a sparkling lake. Listening to the waves on the sandy shore, you continue along the trail.

CONTINUE TO 6.

6. CONTINUE ON THE TRAIL

"Help!"

The peace is interrupted by a distant cry. At first you wonder if it's a trick of the wind, but then you hear the voice again. This time it's clear and desperate. Someone is in trouble! Twisting your ears and straining your eyes, you manage to locate the source of the voice.

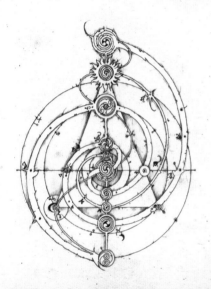

At the edge of the water, a small band of Gelfling is fending off the attacks of a ferocious Aquamander that has slithered out onto the beach. One of the Gelfling is wounded while the other two try to hold off the scaled creature with spears. The Aquamander snatches one of the spears in its jaws and snaps it in half as if it were a twig. The next lunge could easily kill one of the Gelfling, but you're not sure if it's going to attack again. At least, not yet.

THERE'S NO MORE TIME TO WASTE. WHAT DO YOU DO?

TO WAIT TO SEE WHAT THE CREATURE DOES NEXT, GO TO 8.

TO LET OUT A BATTLE CRY AND ATTACK THE BEAST, GO TO 9.

TO HELP THE GELFLING BY TRYING TO RESCUE THE WOUNDED, GO TO 10.

7. FIND YOUR OWN WAY

You inspect the bridge. It's too flimsy to hold your weight. Such is the way of things left alone in the wild. Time and nature are more powerful than any rope or wooden plank. You leave the bridge and the well-marked path behind, forging ahead into the forest. You'll find your own way.

You travel for days and nights, sleeping under the stars and walking by the light of the three suns. The woods are thick and comforting around you.

Your path leads you closer to the mountains, where you walk in their shadow and listen to the echoes whispering from their walls. One morning, you find a tunnel in the mountain face. Wind rushes through it, carrying the song of ocean waves and the scent of the sea.

The sturdy face of the mountain watches as you contemplate entering the tunnel. As you look up at it, you see a footpath snaking up into the heights. Though the woods have ended, the paths of your journey are infinite . . .

TO ENTER THE TUNNEL, GO TO 19.
TO CONTINUE UP THE MOUNTAIN, GO TO 22.

8. WAIT TO SEE THE ODDS

Though you know time is of the essence, you wait. No one ever got ahead by leaping before they looked, and there's no telling what might come next. The most important thing is to calculate the odds before making any decisions. Still, you take out your spear. Just in case.

Your strategy pays off. In a flash of light and a cascading spray of droplets, the beast disappears, diving back into the watery depths. You ask the Gelfling if they need help, but they assure you they'll be fine now the beast is gone. The way ahead is clear, with no further obstacles in your way. With a sigh of relief, you head onward.

CONTINUE TO 11.

9. ATTACK THE BEAST

You grab your spear. There's no time to decide whether or not this is a good idea. With an echoing battle cry, you leap into the fray, your spear clashing with the Aquamander's enormous fangs. It roars, spraying you with spittle that smells of fish, and for an instant you see four rows of teeth rippling down its fleshy gullet.

Then you strike. With a single thrust, your spear's point pierces the Aquamander's soft palate. It flings its head backward, shrieking in pain. You hope that's enough to send the creature back into murky waters. You hold your breath. A moment later, it dives, fleeing into the deep water. The last thing you see is the flip of its finned tail, and then it is gone.

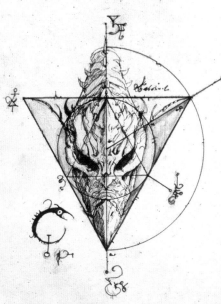

The Gelfling travelers thank you for your help. You learn they were headed to Stone-in-the-Wood, and ask if you might accompany them. They gladly agree, and the four of you return to the trail that winds through the wood.

CONTINUE TO 12.

10. SAVE THE WOUNDED

Knowing the wounded Gelfling is in the most danger, you take your spear and rush in. You toss your dagger to the Gelfling whose spear was destroyed by the Aquamander, focusing your efforts on defending the injured. While the other two fend off the Aquamander, you haul the wounded Gelfling away from the water, into the brush at the perimeter of the beach, where he'll be safe.

By the time you return to the beach, the Aquamander is retreating. When it sees you approaching, its fins flatten in hesitation. A moment later, it dives, fleeing into the deep water. The last thing you see is the flip of its finned tail, and then it is gone.

The Gelfling travelers thank you for your help. You give them a small pouch of healing herbs to treat the injured, and continue on your way.

CONTINUE TO 13.

11. SPRITON

You travel for many days, during which you encounter many challenges. Each time, you weigh the odds and strategize, and each time you make the most of every situation. By the time you reach the sprawling fields south of the Endless Forest, your shoulders are strong from carrying your pack. As you watch the wild Landstriders gallop across the land, your mind is focused, fortified with the many lessons you have learned.

A small wood is visible from atop the hill where you stand, and you make your way toward it. As the shadow of the trees cools your back, you breathe in the scent of the forest and feel a calm relief.

The trees part, revealing a cluster of Gelfling homes encircling a central hearth. You nod to yourself. It is not by chance or luck that you have arrived here. You knew that you would find your way if the timing was right. And so, finally, you've come home to Sami Thicket, home of the Spriton.

SPRITON CLAN CHARACTERISTICS

- INDEPENDENT
- HARDWORKING
- STRATEGIC
- SELFISH
- PARTICULAR
- OLD-FASHIONED

12. STONEWOOD

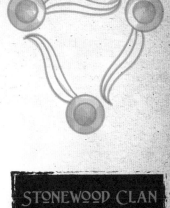

You accompany the travelers through the wood, exchanging songs to help the time pass. The companionship makes the journey so easy, you feel as if you could walk forever, so long as you have friends by your side.

You find the trail to be better marked as you follow it deeper into the Endless Forest. Pillars of stones and staffs with banners line the trailside, and soon you see wheel ruts from wagons in the packed soil. Through the trees you hear the clanging of blacksmith hammers and Gelfling voices.

The woods open into a large green clearing. Dozens and dozens of Gelfling homes populate the place, built into the rocks and trees, adorned with carved stone and enormous shells. Gelfling are everywhere, and you even spot a rolling ball of fur—a Fizzgig! With joy in your heart, you realize you've finally made it to Stone-in-the-Wood, home of the Stonewood.

STONEWOOD CLAN CHARACTERISTICS

- INDUSTRIOUS
- PROUD
- CONFIDENT
- SINGLE-MINDED
- HAUGHTY
- BRASH

13. DRENCHEN

Though you follow the marked trail for a time, eventually your feet and heart urge you away from it, into the wood. You feel more at home among the trees and the hundreds of creatures living within them.

You can taste moisture in the air, and follow your ears to a river. Its waters are cool and sparkling, so clear that you can see the smoothed stones lining the riverbed. You stop to take a drink, letting the refreshing water run down your arms and over your face. The water gives you life, and you let it nourish you.

You follow the river for days and days, through wood and field and highland. When you feel weary, the river is always there to revitalize you. You travel until the air grows warm and thick, the trees stretching higher than ever before. When your path finally ends, it is at the foot of a giant tree. Gelfling homes are nestled within its bark and branches, safe and protected. You let out a sigh of relief; you've finally come to Great Smerth in the Swamp of Sog, home of the Drenchen.

DRENCHEN CLAN CHARACTERISTICS

- SOCIAL
- INTUITIVE
- CARING
- SELF-CENTERED
- STUBBORN
- SELF-IMPORTANT

14. SIFA

You put out the fire and follow the trail of smoke. As you approach the endless rolling waves of the ocean, you realize there is a ship out on the water. It comes closer, called by the smoke from your fire. It is a small Sifan vessel, with crimson sails and purple and blue flags. The Gelfling aboard call to you. When asked where you are headed, you can only point to the moons. The Sifan sailors nod with understanding and beckon to you.

"Then come with us, and we'll sail until we reach the edge of Thra!" they cry.

The call of the moons is quiet, but undeniable. Setting your sights on their serene silver faces, you set forth in pursuit. Days pass as you sail across the sea. And yet, you never tire of the journey, for you can always see the moons guiding you. Even during the day. You become close with the Sifan crew. Close enough to be family. One morning you awaken aboard the ship as it rocks in place on the waves, and realize you are home.

SIFA CLAN CHARACTERISTICS

- **INTUITIVE**
- **ADVENTUROUS**
- **SPIRITUAL**
- **SPONTANEOUS**
- **SUPERSTITIOUS**
- **MATERIALISTIC**

15. DOUSAN

The desert calls to you in its silent, haunting voice.

The shifting crystal sands make every step difficult, but you know that if you stop walking, you will sink until you are swallowed. You keep a steady pace, conserving your energy as much as possible. You know that this is not a journey of destination, but one of transformation.

With only your thoughts and will to guide you, you walk until the desert surrounds you on every side. It seems endless, dazzling even at night, the dunes broken by the crystal reefs and the occasional flurry of sparkling sand. Bony creatures adapted to survive the arid place scurry across your path at night, when the light of the three suns isn't blinding against the sand.

DOUSAN CLAN CHARACTERISTICS

- **TRADITIONAL**
- **INTROSPECTIVE**
- **SPIRITUAL**
- **LONELY**
- **FATALISTIC**
- **ALOOF**

On the horizon, Crystal Skimmers skip along the dunes like fish on waves. On their backs are Gelfling in brilliant indigo and crimson cloaks. They see you. You see them. You climb aboard one of the Skimmers and feel the lurch of the deck as it launches into flight. In no time you arrive in a lush oasis hidden in a valley in the red Claw Mountains—the Wellspring. You turn to your companions as the Skimmer slows, and you realize they are the Dousan, and they've brought you home.

16. GROTTAN

Your path takes you through every mountain pass and along the most scenic ridges. It seems as if all of Thra is laid out before you, an infinite garden of adventurous possibilities. It's hard to believe that you have never left home before, and now that you have, you can't wait to absorb everything you see and hear and smell.

After many days, just as you feel you may have seen it all, you come across the entrance to a cave, hidden by trees and fallen rocks. The shadows that fill the cave are heavy with mystery, and something deep in your heart pulls you into them. You're excited to see where this new path leads, and what interesting and wonderful places are yet to be discovered beneath the mountains.

GROTTAN CLAN CHARACTERISTICS

- **INTUITIVE**
- **INTROSPECTIVE**
- **OPTIMISTIC**
- **NAIVE**
- **SHELTERED**
- **HUMBLE**

The tunnel is lit with glow moss and dimly glowing crystal veins, blue and white and lovely. The sound of water dripping, along with gentle gusts of fresh air, leads you through a maze of tunnels . . . until suddenly, the walls widen and you find yourself standing in an echoing cavern. Gelfling homes are carved into every face of the rock, and the sound of music and the crackling of a hearth fire are comforting to your ears.

This is the place your path brought you, and you wouldn't have wanted it any other way. You've finally come to Domrak, deep in the Caves of Grot, home of the Grottan Gelfling.

17. VAPRA

Your quest to reach the highest peak brings you all the way north of the Endless Forest, where the mountains turn blue and white in the cold, snow-covered north. You cut your path alone, relying on your own tried-and-true knowledge of both the world and the creatures within it. When you climb the peak of the mountain, you find yourself looking down on the Silver Sea as snow falls gently across your shoulders. You have finally proven yourself.

Sparkling below is a beautiful city, like a crystal of ice shining in the snow. After your long journey, you could use a rest. Warmth and a hot mug of ta while making your final journal entries, perhaps. You trudge through the snow, descending into cobbled streets with dome-roofed Gelfling homes. It feels welcoming to you, as if it has been waiting for you. As if it is a place worthy of you, and you of it.

You realize with a start that you've finally come home, to Ha'rar, the home of the Vapra, and seat of the Gelfling throne.

VAPRA CLAN CHARACTERISTICS

- **RESOURCEFUL**
- **NOBLE**
- **ACADEMIC**
- **COMPETITIVE**
- **ENTITLED**
- **PRETENTIOUS**

18. GO TO THE DESERT

You follow the trail. It skirts the border of the desert, where the crystal sands ebb lazily like the waves of the ocean at low tide. Before long, you see the trees of the Endless Forest ahead. The foot trail curves away from the desert and into the forest. It is well marked with stones, welcoming and safe.

But the Crystal Desert beckons you with every glittering flash of light. Its haunting silence whispers to you, promising to unlock the mysteries of the universe and answer questions you've never thought to ask. Though it may be dangerous and lonely, many have survived within the Crystal Desert's fierce embrace. Perhaps you be one of them . . . or perhaps it's safer to return to the woods.

TO FOLLOW THE PATH BACK INTO THE WOODS, GO TO 6.
TO GO OUT INTO THE DESERT, GO TO 15.

19. GO TO THE SEA

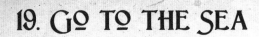

You reach the sea. Travelers' lanterns stud the long strip of black sand, illuminating a winding trail with their flickering lights. A makeshift firepit is at your feet, dug by some previous traveler and lined with stones. The ashes have long gone cold, but you know you could easily find driftwood and light it once more.

TO LIGHT A FIRE AND ASK THE FLAMES, GO TO 20.

20. CONSULT THE FLAMES

When faced with an unanswerable question, the songs have always told of Gelfling finding answers in the flames. Perhaps now is a time to explore this tradition of your ancestors. You comb the beach, returning to the small firepit dug in the cold sand with an armful of dried driftwood. Using a piece of flint left in the pit, along with a knife from your traveling pack, you light a modest fire.

The flames are warm and comforting, though they eat through the driftwood so quickly, it won't be long before they go out.

You gaze into the mesmerizing tongues of gold and amber as a thin tail of smoke winds into the sky. You open your mind, as if you might dreamfast with the fire itself. You wait for it to tell you its secrets.

The flames bend in a small gust of wind, and the thread of gray smoke tilts toward the sea . . .

CONTINUE TO 14.

21. FOCUSED ON THE JOURNEY

The air thins as you hike higher into the mountains. Every gnarled tree and tangle of finger-vines adds color and interest to the journey. A small flock of Z'nid birds flutter overhead, and the clouds pass lazily in long, gauzy streaks. You go where your feet take you, where you feel called. Although you walk alone, you do not feel lonely.

Of a thousand trails, this is the one you chose, and you can't help but feel it was meant to be. The journey itself is its own reward.

CONTINUE TO 16.

22. FOCUSED ON YOUR DESTINATION

The narrow mountain trail is rugged, testing both your resourcefulness and endurance. You keep up with it, but only barely—the trail itself is your only companion, beside you every step of the way, challenging you with its friendly rivalry. For every waypoint you pass, you find another. Your eyes are always set on the next goal.

After a day's hike, you reach a high peak from which you can see all the land below. But you aren't done yet. Only now can you see the blue mountains to the north. Taller and more jagged, and even more daunting. A new rival and a new invitation.

Eyes set on your destination, you trek onward.

CONTINUE TO 17.

WHICH SPECIES OF THRA ARE YOU MOST LIKE?

Thra is a place of wonder, populated by innumerable creatures. Some live peacefully with one another, while others may be more solitary. Look into the Crystal. Look into yourself. Which of these iconic creatures of Thra do you see?

WOULD YOU RATHER?
EAT A LIVE CRAWLIE OR A ROASTED NEBRIE?

1 WHEN I HAVE A DAY OFF, I PREFER TO SPEND IT . . .

A — Reading a book or listening to a podcast—any activity that teaches me something new or sharpens my understanding of what I already know.

B — In the garden. There's nothing better than being outside and surrounded by nature.

C — Spending time with friends. Being social helps me recharge, even if it's just hanging out and playing board games.

D — With some me-time. I have a lot to think about, questions to answer, puzzles to solve . . . and being around other people doesn't help!

2 WHEN MEETING SOMEONE FOR THE FIRST TIME, I . . .

A — Don't mind doing most of the talking. I find that talking about myself helps people open up more in a conversation. Plus, I have some great stories to tell!

B — Let them do most of the talking. I prefer to learn more about other people before sharing about myself.

C — Ask a lot of questions and focus on the things we have in common. And I'll try to get a joke in there if I can—humor always helps ease along new friendships!

D — Stare at them until they ask whatever question they want to ask. I don't have time for small talk.

3 I WOULD DESCRIBE MYSELF AS . . .

A Confident and knowledgeable in most topics, and an expert in my field of choice, within which I am unparalleled.

B Humble and hardworking—I worked hard for what I've earned in life.

C Loving and warm—it's important to me that I treat others as I would want to be treated.

D Old and jaded, but that's what happens when you've been around as long as I have. Seen what I've seen.

4 IF A FRIEND OF MINE WAS HAVING A HARD TIME, I WOULD . . .

A Offer advice based on my previous experiences. Perhaps they could use that information to improve their own circumstances.

B Ask them what they need. Everyone needs different things during difficult times, and I wouldn't want to assume that our needs were the same.

C Cook for them. Food heals the body and the soul at the same time!

D Look to the stars for answers. The movement of the spheres, the suns, and the moons—I'm sure the answers are there, somewhere! Just might take a while to find them.

5 I WOULD SAY MY GREATEST FEAR IS . . .

A Not being my true self. There is a side of me that I don't openly share. Because I have that secret side, I fear I may never truly develop close relationships with others.

B Being alone. If I didn't have my friends and family, I wouldn't know what to do with myself.

C Sadness. I don't know what to do when I'm feeling sad. I'd rather just be happy all the time!

D Being forgotten. There was a time when I might not have felt that way, but these days I wonder if it's a destiny that's already sealed.

6 I WOULD SAY MY GREATEST STRENGTH IS . . .

A My mental capacity and experience. I have lived a long time and seen many things. More than most, in fact.

B My persistence. A tree doesn't grow overnight, and neither will I. But with time, water, sun, and earth, I know I can flourish.

C My optimism. A positive outlook can change even the worst of circumstances into something that can be overcome. One must always have hope.

D Can't remember. Might have been my memory, once, but not anymore! HA!

ANSWER KEY

IF YOU ANSWERED MOSTLY A's, YOU'RE MOST LIKE A SKEKSIS OR MYSTIC!

Wise with ancient knowledge from a world they left behind, the Skeksis and Mystics are two halves of a greater whole. Those who are most like the Skeksis and Mystics may find themselves torn between two contrasting feelings—either acting impulsively or overthinking things. They enjoy honing specific skills, and usually express themselves wholly through a particular hobby or interest, be it engineering, philosophy, or music. If you arrived at this outcome, you might benefit from seeking balance as an alternative to juggling conflicting emotions or desires.

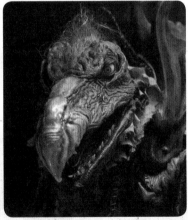

CURIOUS ABOUT WHETHER YOU'RE MORE LIKE A MYSTIC OR A SKEKSIS? TURN TO PAGE 38 TO FIND OUT.

IF YOU ANSWERED MOSTLY B's, YOU'RE MOST LIKE A GELFLING!

Close to nature and in tune with the Song of Thra, the Gelfling flourished for many trine prior to the arrival of the Skeksis and the Mystics. Those who are most like Gelfling find comfort in the natural beauty of the world, preferring to spend most of their time outdoors and tending to the many plants and creatures of the land. While usually social, they can also be clannish, proud, and competitive. If you arrived at this outcome, you might benefit from trying to find common ground with others rather than viewing them as rivals.

INTERESTED IN FINDING OUT WHICH CLAN WOULD BE A GOOD FIT FOR YOU? TURN TO PAGE 6 TO BEGIN YOUR JOURNEY!

IF YOU ANSWERED MOSTLY C's, YOU'RE MOST LIKE A PODLING!

Living day by day and taking joy in the simple pleasures of life, Podlings are not the kind to stress over abstract ideas or concepts. Those who are most like Podlings tend to be easygoing, and thanks to their even-keeled personalities, make reliable and stable friends. And they throw a great party! They enjoy domestic activities and find it easy to get along with just about anybody, and always know how to lighten the mood when necessary—perhaps, sometimes, to a fault. If you arrived at this outcome, you might benefit from taking the time to explore beyond your comfort zone. It can be good to try new things once in a while!

WANT TO TEST YOUR PODLING LANGUAGE SKILLS? TURN TO PAGE 60 TO SEE HOW FLUENT YOU ARE!

IF YOU ANSWERED MOSTLY D's, YOU'RE MOST LIKE AUGHRA!

The only one of her kind, Aughra was born when the world of Thra wished to have eyes to see and a mouth to speak. Those who are most like Aughra have seen it all—and learned from it, though how to apply this wisdom is still anyone's guess. Thousands of trine have left Aughra somewhat disheveled and disoriented, but so it goes for any creature who has turned her last remaining eye to the stars for so long. If you arrived at this outcome, you might benefit from taking a moment to be more present in the here and now. Look at what's going on around you, and you just might learn something!

WOULD YOU RATHER?

ARM-WRESTLE A SILK SPITTER OR RACE A LANDSTRIDER?

ARE YOU MORE LIKE A MYSTIC OR A SKEKSIS?

Once a single entity, now the Skeksis and the Mystics live separately, but with hearts and minds intertwined. The Skeksis reside in the Castle of the Crystal, where they rule over all of Thra and hold the Crystal of Truth captive. The Mystics have scattered to the winds in search of the greater wisdom known only by the suns and the moons themselves. Two halves of a once whole—ambitious Skeksis or gentle Mystic—do you resemble one of these ancient, powerful creatures?

1 WHEN FACED WITH A PROBLEM, I'M MORE LIKELY TO . . .

A   Work on it tirelessly until I've solved it.

B   Set it aside and wait until the solution comes to me.

2 WHEN MEETING NEW PEOPLE FOR THE FIRST TIME, I'M . . .

A   Talkative and energetic.

B   Anecdotal and inquisitive.

3 WHEN I GO GROCERY SHOPPING, I TYPICALLY . . .

A   Buy whatever I'm hungry for.

B   Make a list beforehand and stick to it.

4 IF I FOUND OUT MY FRIENDS WERE TALKING ABOUT ME BEHIND MY BACK . . .

A   I wouldn't be surprised. I talk about them behind *their* backs, after all.

B   I'd shrug it off. What others say about me doesn't bother me.

5 IN MY FREE TIME I LIKE TO . . .

A Make progress on one of my hundreds of projects. I have to keep busy!

B Take things slowly. Sometimes it's nice to do nothing at all and be present in the moment.

6 I PREFER . . .

A Coffee.

B Tea.

7 WHEN I FORGET TO DO SOMETHING, I . . .

A Get very angry, but I'm great at coming up with excuses!

B Try not to worry about it. I'll probably forget I forgot soon enough.

8 IF I COULD HAVE ANY MAGICAL POWER, IT WOULD BE . . .

A To remain strong and beautiful forever.

B To remain wise and contemplative forever.

9 WHEN I GET TOGETHER WITH MY FRIENDS, I . . .

A Like to go out and do something exciting and adventurous.

B Prefer to stay in and discuss a book we've all read.

10 MY FAVORITE THING ABOUT TRYING NEW THINGS IS . . .

A The sense of pride and thrill of accomplishment.

B Knowing I've learned something new.

11 WHEN SINGING WITH FRIENDS, I . . .

A Take the lead.

B Join the chorus.

ANSWER KEY

IF YOU ANSWERED MOSTLY A's, YOU'RE MORE LIKE A SKEKSIS!

Ambitious and intelligent, crafty and sometimes a bit impulsive, you're more like a Skeksis! Skeksis know how to start things and get them done, even if it means making a few enemies along the way. They're very social and love a good party, especially if it gives them a chance to gossip among themselves to get the latest dirt.

IF YOU ANSWERED MOSTLY B's, YOU'RE MORE LIKE A MYSTIC!

Thoughtful and in the moment, peaceful but occasionally sluggish, you're more like a Mystic! Mystics take their time understanding the world around them, philosophizing their way through life—so much so that sometimes they forget to actually *do* anything. They're very in tune with nature, and spend most of their days asking questions and waiting for the answers.

How Well Do You Know the Skeksis and the Mystics?

Despite their current state, the Skeksis were not always cruel and merciless. Some were gregarious and outgoing, while others preferred to keep their secrets in solitude. But time and power corrupted the hearts and minds of the Skeksis lords, turning their intelligence to suspicion and their ambition into bloodthirsty competition.

After the separation, the Mystics scattered themselves across Thra, rarely gathering in one place. They became hermits and wanderers, absorbing what wisdom they could from the world, and returning it to the many creatures, including the Gelfling, they encountered. Now they are rarely seen, nothing but myths to even the Skeksis with whom they are intertwined . . .

1 **WHICH MYSTIC HELPED AUGHRA REMEMBER THE SONG OF THRA?**

A urVa the Archer
B urSol the Chanter
C urSu the Master
D urTih the Alchemist

2 **WHICH SKEKSIS HAS A MECHANICAL EYE?**

A skekTek the Scientist
B skekOk the Scroll-Keeper
C skekZok the Ritual Master
D skekLach the Collector

WOULD YOU RATHER?

BECOME A SERVANT OF THE SKEKSIS OR A PUPIL OF THE MYSTICS?

3 SKEKSIL IS THE NAME OF WHICH SKEKSIS?

A   The Emperor

B   The Gourmand

C   The Chamberlain

D   The Treasurer

4 WHICH SKEKSIS WAS ONCE KNOWN AS THE CONQUEROR?

A   skekNa the Slave Master

B   skekEkt the Ornamentalist

C   skekVar the General

D   skekGra the Heretic

5 WHICH SKEKSIS IS URVA THE ARCHER'S COUNTERPART?

A   skekSo the Emperor

B   skekMal the Hunter

C   skekSil the Chamberlain

D   skekVar the General

6 URGOH THE WANDERER IS THE MYSTIC COUNTERPART TO WHICH SKEKSIS?

A   skekMal the Hunter

B   skekOk the Scroll-Keeper

C   skekGra the Heretic

D   skekSil the Chamberlain

7 WHICH SKEKSIS IS RESPONSIBLE FOR DIVIDING THE SEVEN CLANS OF THE GELFLING?

A   skekSil the Chamberlain

B   skekSo the Emperor

C   skekTek the Scientist

D   skekMal the Hunter

8 WHAT IS THE PROPER NAME FOR THE MYSTIC RACE?

A skekRu

B urSis

C urSkek

D urRu

9 WHICH SKEKSIS IS RESPONSIBLE FOR DEFENDING THE SKEKSIS CASTLE?

A skekVar the General

B skekMal the Hunter

C skekOk the Scroll-Keeper

D skekTek the Scientist

WOULD YOU RATHER?

SPEND A NIGHT IN THE CAVES OF GROT OR THE VAPRAN LIBRARY?

1 URVA THE ARCHER.

A This Mystic made it his duty to seek out Aughra and give her the guidance she needs to remember the Song of Thra and open the dreamspace where she can call upon the Gelfling. Once that mission is complete, the Archer is to go on to work out how he might defeat his dark half, the Hunter.

2 SKEKTEK THE SCIENTIST.

A Despite his brilliance when it comes to technology and experimentation, his arrogance can cause him to be overconfident. Thanks to him, the Emperor decides it was his fault the vial of Gelfling essence was stolen, and his eye was eaten by a Peeper Beetle as punishment.

3 THE CHAMBERLAIN.

C It is the Chamberlain's job to serve the Emperor's best interests, of course while serving his own as often as possible. The Chamberlain oversees the Emperor's affairs and makes sure his will is carried out. In the past, he has always been the Emperor's favorite, but lately things have changed . . .

4 SKEKGRA THE HERETIC.

D He was once a warlord who voyaged far and wide, claiming land in the name of skekSo the Emperor. He was feared by all, Skeksis and Gelfling alike. But in his travels, he came across a prophecy telling of a Conjunction. After that, he was not the same, and left the Skeksis' castle to pursue answers.

5 B SKEKMAL THE HUNTER

Though vastly different in temperament, the Hunter and the Archer are both expert trackers and survivalists. Once they have their sights set on a goal, they are unerring in their path to obtain it. However, while the Archer is focused on helping Aughra unite the Gelfling, the Hunter has pooled every effort into preventing it. His goal is to capture and destroy Rian, and he won't stop until he's done it!

6 C SKEKGRA THE HERETIC

Independently of skekGra the Heretic, urGoh the Wanderer discovered the prophecy of the Conjunction and embarked on a quest to find his Skeksis counterpart. When the two found each other, they realized they truly were connected—two halves of what was once the same being.

7
B
SKEKSo THE EMPEROR. Early on, when he realized the Gelfling could potentially overpower the Skeksis if they unified, the Emperor made sure to keep the clans divided and in conflict with one another. He even made the decision to favor the Vapra over the other clans, naming their maudra the All-Maudra, all in an effort to keep the Gelfling clans weak and fragmented.

8
D
URRU. Though they are often called Mystics, these gentle creatures that represent the light half to the Skeksis dark half are called urRu. When the names of the urRu and the Skeksis are combined, they form the names of the urSkeks: the original species that arrived on Thra and was later split in two by the light of the three suns and the Crystal.

9
A
SKEKVAR THE GENERAL. Originally, skekVar's role was to defend the castle and command the garrison. However, with the Gelfling rebellion came changes within the Skeksis ranks, and skekVar suddenly found himself in a rather advantageous position among the other lords. Could his brute-force approach to stopping the Gelfling finally get him the Emperor's favor?

WHAT GELFLING OCCUPATION SUITS YOU BEST?

The number of Gelfling occupations is as diverse and interesting as the Gelfling clans themselves. Answer the following questions to find out which of the most popular Gelfling roles might be a good fit for you!

1 A GROUP OF PEOPLE ARE PLANNING A SURPRISE PARTY FOR A FRIEND. HOW DO YOU GET INVOLVED?

A   Get involved? I'm planning and coordinating the whole thing!

B   I'm the one in charge of getting the friend to the party without spoiling the surprise.

C   I'll be reading up on the friend's star sign to pick out the best gift.

D   I'm in the band! I've been practicing the guest of honor's favorite songs.

2 WHAT'S SOMETHING YOU STRUGGLE WITH ON A REGULAR BASIS?

A   Loneliness. Sometimes I feel like I can't share my feelings with others for fear they might lose their trust in me.

B   Finding time to relax. It's hard to practice self-care when I spend all my energy caring for others.

C   Making friends. Sometimes I struggle to express myself in a way that other people can understand.

D   Discerning the truth. It can be frustrating when people tell stories with conflicting information.

3 HOW DO YOU OVERCOME CHALLENGES AND OBSTACLES?

A Take a step back and make a plan, then ask for help from others.

B I always prioritize assets and minimize risk. Better safe than sorry.

C I follow my intuition— I'm usually right.

D I think about how others have overcome the same challenges in the past, and build on those lessons with my own insight.

4 WHAT WOULD YOUR FRIENDS SAY ABOUT YOU?

A That I'm confident.

B That I'm reliable.

C That I'm intuitive.

D That I'm intelligent.

WOULD YOU RATHER?
HAVE THE GELFLING ABILITY TO HEAL OR DREAMFAST?

ANSWER KEY

IF YOU ANSWERED MOSTLY A's, YOU'RE A LEADER!

You're confident and a natural when it comes to gaining the trust and respect of others. You're not afraid to go first into danger, and know how important it is to show strength and bravery when others are looking to you for guidance. Popular Gelfling leaders include maudras (clan matriarchs) and leaders of the Gelfling resistance. Notable Gelfling leaders include Rian, Maudra Argot, Maudra Fara, Ordon, and Naia.

IF YOU ANSWERED MOSTLY B's, YOU'RE A PROTECTOR!

You're courageous and always looking out for those less fortunate than you. Others find you easy to talk to, and often come to you for help. They know you'll never let them down! You are resourceful and reliable. Popular Gelfling protectors include farmers, shepherds, Castle Guards, Vapran paladins, and clan warriors. Notable Gelfling protectors include Deet, Gurjin, Mira, and Tavra. (Don't forget one notable Podling protector—Hup!)

IF YOU ANSWERED MOSTLY C's, YOU'RE A SAGE!

You're intuitive and know how to listen closely to the voice of Thra, whether through the signs of the weather or the mystical symbols within far-dreams. You are comfortable facing the unknown, willing to push into the mysteries of the universe in search of secrets. Popular Gelfling sages include Dousan sandmasters, far-dreamers, and oracles. Notable Gelfling sages include Onica, Rek'yr, and Elder Cadia.

WOULD YOU RATHER?
OBEY THE SKEKSIS OR JOIN THE GELFLING RESISTANCE?

IF YOU ANSWERED MOSTLY D's, YOU'RE A HISTORIAN!

You're academic and have a fine memory for stories and songs of the past, finding yourself enraptured by the tales told of adventuring Gelfling of yore. You believe understanding the past is the best way of finding your way in the future. Popular Gelfling historians include librarians, song tellers, and dream-stitchers. Notable Gelfling historians include Brea, Kylan, and the Librarian.

WOULD YOU RATHER?
SPEND YOUR LIFE TRAINING TO BE
ALL-MAUDRA OR SPEND A YEAR
WITH THE ORDER OF LESSER SERVICE?

WHAT THRA CRITTER ARE YOU MOST LIKE?

Thra is populated by thousands of creatures, big and small, with a vast array of temperaments and personalities. Many Gelfling use creatures as metaphors for personality types. So, which are you? Ferocious as a Fizzgig or slow as a flat-footed Nebrie? Take this quiz to find out!

1 IN A STRESSFUL SITUATION, HOW DO YOU REACT?

A   I amp myself up—I can handle any problem!

B   I panic! I don't like to be stressed out.

C   I stay cool and ride the wave.

D   I make a plan and execute it. Simple as that.

2 WHAT WORD WOULD YOUR FRIENDS USE TO DESCRIBE YOU?

A   Energetic

B   Silly

C   Cool

D   Strong

3 WHAT KINDS OF FOODS DO YOU PREFER?

A   Spicy

B   Sweet

C   Salty

D   Bitter

4 AFTER A LONG DAY, HOW DO YOU UNWIND?

A   Play video games with my friends all night.

B   Cuddle up with a good book and a mug of tea.

C   Sit on the porch with my favorite beverage and people-watch.

D   Go for a run.

5 I WOULD SAY MY GREATEST STRENGTH IS . . .

A My vitality. I'm always ready to go!

B My optimism. I can always find the silver lining.

C My adaptability. I can always find a way to make things work.

D My intelligence. I can always think of a better way.

6 I LIKE TO SPEND MY SCHOOL RECESS . . .

A Horsing around and getting into trouble.

B Sitting in the shade with a snack.

C Hanging out and talking with friends.

D Playing competitive sports.

7 WHEN FACED WITH A DIFFICULT PROJECT, I . . .

A Get frustrated easily, but complete it with sheer willpower.

B Take my time. Even if it's not perfect, at least I tried!

C Ask for help, and see if anyone has useful advice.

D Take a step back to look at the project logically and strategically.

8 MY FAVORITE KIND OF MUSIC IS . . .

A Bouncy and fun.

B Acoustic and playful.

C Fast-paced and invigorating.

D Lyrically strong and poetic.

WOULD YOU RATHER?

SHARE YOUR HOUSE WITH ONE SKEKSIS OR ONE HUNDRED PODLINGS?

IF YOU ANSWERED MOSTLY A's, YOU'RE MOST LIKE A FIZZGIG!

Fizzgigs are rowdy, energetic little furballs notorious for their rambunctious shenanigans in the wood and among Gelfling communities. They're social and love to play and make noise—if there's a Fizzgig in the area, you'll hear it sooner or later. If someone says you're *ferocious as a Fizzgig,* they mean it as a compliment, though they might be teasing just a little about your bark being bigger than your bite!

IF YOU ANSWERED MOSTLY B's, YOU'RE MOST LIKE A NEBRIE!

Nebries are giant, friendly grubs that live in swamps and wetlands, feeding primarily on algae and decaying plant life on the forest floor. They never stop feeding, and they never stop growing. Those that are similar to Nebries are methodical and easygoing. Some may call someone a Nebrie to indicate that they're slowpokes, but more frequently being likened to a *happy Nebrie* means someone is as content as can be.

IF YOU ANSWERED MOSTLY C's, YOU'RE MOST LIKE A CRYSTAL SKIMMER!

Crystal Skimmers are social creatures that travel the Crystal Desert in huge family groups called pods. Although Skimmers are herbivorous and nonviolent, due to their size they have no predators in the desert and flourish peacefully. Those that are similar to Crystal Skimmers are adaptable and confident. If someone says you're *swimming like a Skimmer,* they mean you're going with the flow—staying calm even during stressful situations.

WOULD YOU RATHER?
BELIEVE IN PROPHECIES OR MAKE YOUR OWN FATE?

IF YOU ANSWERED MOSTLY D's, YOU'RE MOST LIKE A LANDSTRIDER!

Noble and fearless, Landstriders are masters of the plains and the woods alike. The only terrain they don't favor is the shifting seas of the Crystal Desert. Their speed is only matched by their courage. Those that are similar to Landstriders feel comfortable living life at a quick pace and perform well under pressure. If someone says you're *leggy as a Landstrider,* they mean you're efficient and hardworking, and won't back down until the job is done!

TEST YOUR PODLING LANGUAGE SKILLS!

Podlings have lived in harmony with the Gelfling for as long as anyone can remember. Whether you are Spriton or Vapra, you have probably picked up a few Podling phrases here and there; any self-respecting traveler knows that Podlings always have the best traveling routes and the most relaxing waypoints.

Here are some helpful phrases when traveling.

My name is ____.	Apada ____.
Nice to meet you.	Fala avo.
What's your name?	Otamvam?
Pardon me.	Dzonla temar.
You're welcome.	Trabom.
See you later. / Goodbye.	Zodzenpo.

THINK YOU'RE FLUENT IN PODLING? NOW'S THE TIME TO TEST YOUR SKILLS.

1 WHAT DOES "ADUMA" MEAN?

A Mother

B Monster

C Many

2 HOW DO YOU SAY "NO" IN PODLING?

A Ne

B Nein

C Da

3 WHAT IS THE PODLING WORD FOR "PODLING"?

A Apopiapod

B Apipipod

C Apopopiadod

4 HOW DO YOU SAY "THANK YOU" IN PODLING?

A Fala avopo

B Fala shi

C Fala vam

WOULD YOU RATHER? STAY IN ONE PLACE SURROUNDED BY MATERIAL COMFORTS OR TRAVEL THE WORLD WITH VERY FEW BELONGINGS?

ANSWER KEY 1.B. Monster 2.A. Ne 3.A. Apopiapod 4.B. Fala vam

WHAT'S YOUR GELFLING STAR SIGN?

Each of Thra's nine greater seasons, called ninets, are represented by a constellation that can be found prominently in the night sky during that season. It is said that the constellation under which one is born can say a lot about a Gelfling.

The following star signs have been calculated according to the Gregorian Earth calendar. What does your Gelfling star sign say about you?

YESMIT (AUGHRA'S EYE)
JANUARY 3–FEBRUARY 12

Those born under the star of Yesmit, Aughra's Eye, are known to be both intuitive and pragmatic. They may often see things others cannot. Because of their wide-open "third eye," those born under the star of Yesmit may also become mentally exhausted, frequently erecting emotional and spiritual barriers to give themselves reprieve. Yesmits will find relationship success with Tras and Ioles, whose quiet natures do not crowd the Yesmit's overactive mind. Avoid Eopis and Soushis.

EOPI (THE FIZZGIG)
FEBRUARY 13–MARCH 24

Those born under the star of Eopi, the Fizzgig, are blessed with boundless energy. They frequently find success in athletic professions or those careers that require strength and stamina. They can be friendly and charismatic, though sometimes their zest for life and extroversion make them overly competitive. Those born under the star of Eopi may find more success mingling with others of similar natures, such as Sucos and Obers. Avoid Ioles.

ARMIGO (THE UNAMOTH CHRYSALIS)
MARCH 25–MAY 3

Those born under the sign of the Unamoth Chrysalis, Armigo, are natural poets able to see beauty everywhere they look. Like the pupas that represent them, they can be quite reclusive and often need time alone in order to develop their thoughts and feelings. However, when they finally emerge from their stasis, they can be quite social, often taking the spotlight with their refreshed radiance. Armigos find solid friends in Tras and Ioles, and should avoid Yesmits.

OBER (THE HOLLERBAT)
MAY 4–JUNE 13

Like the Hollerbat that represents them, those born under the star of Ober are known for their animated, enthusiastic personalities, which often make them the life of the party. However, for all their gregarious behavior, they are the sign that may value solitude the most. Obers take pleasure in activities that are short lived but active, and while they can be spontaneous, it is equally as important for them to find time to recover from their rigorous activities. Obers will enjoy the active, energetic company of Eopis, though they may find better long-term relationships with Ioles.

TRA (THE TRIANGLE, OR *FIRCA*)
JUNE 14–JULY 24

Those born under the star of Tra, the Triangle (sometimes called the *Firca*), are blessed with completely balanced energy. They are often equally comfortable in large groups or on their own, depending on their mood. Those born under this sign are also likely to take interest in wide and diverse topics. Sometimes, these interests can be too different from one another, dividing a Tra's attention until it is too thin to be effective. Those born under this sign will find rewarding companionships with Yesmits and Armigos. Avoid Rijos.

WOULD YOU RATHER?
BE ABLE TO FLY LIKE BREA OR BREATHE UNDERWATER LIKE NAIA?

SOUSHI (THE ROPE-WEAVER)
JULY 25–SEPTEMBER 2

Those born under the star of Soushi, the Rope-Weaver, are both blessed and cursed with an acute attention to detail. This makes them successful in careers and activities involving fine and meticulous work, though their desire for perfection may also cause them frequent stress during the same activities. Soushis are not particularly social, preferring fewer but very intimate relationships. They get along best with Armigos and Sucos, but should avoid Yesmits.

IOLE (THE STONE)
SEPTEMBER 3–OCTOBER 13

Those born under the star of Iole, the Stone, are steadfast, consistent people who flourish in both social and solitary scenarios thanks to their strong understanding of self. Ioles may not seem to be the most intuitive types at first, but their groundedness is seated in a long history of personal introspection. Ioles prefer to take their time with every task, and may become easily flustered or confused if ambushed by more spontaneous activities. Thus, it is recommended Ioles seek out the company of Yesmits and Armigos. Avoid Eopis.

WOULD YOU RATHER?

BECOME WISE OR BECOME POWERFUL?

WOULD YOU RATHER?

LISTEN TO SOMEONE ELSE TELL A SONG OR TELL YOUR OWN TO OTHERS?

SUCO (THE SPOON)
OCTOBER 14–NOVEMBER 23

Those born under the star of Suco, the Spoon, are characterized by warm and supportive natures. Even those who have not yet refined or trained their skills will still often find themselves in caretaking roles. The Sucos' benevolent personality is balanced by their simple, blunt commitment to the truth—much like the rap of a wooden spoon across the knuckles. Because they spend much of their time taking care of others, Sucos would do best to find companionship in Eopis and Soushis. They should avoid Armigos.

RIJO (THE RIVER)
NOVEMBER 24–JANUARY 2

Like the winding Black River, those born under the star of Rijo are always in motion, whether physically or mentally. They find it difficult to be still. However, this transitional way of life means that they are often able to finish what they start, even if it takes a while. The Rijo may find satisfaction in careers that are not repetitive and that involve travel. In relationships, they should seek out those who do not mind their fluid energy, such as Sucos and Armigos. Avoid those that prefer more stable energy, such as Tras.

WHICH MAUDRA ARE YOU MOST LIKE?

The maudras of the seven clans may all have the same role, to protect and lead their clans, but they each have very different styles. Which maudra are you most like?

1 WHEN DEALING WITH AN UNRULY YOUTH, WHAT APPROACH WOULD YOU TAKE?

A I don't often have time to handle youngsters that aren't my own. Off to the Order of Lesser Service!

B A stern talking-to often does the trick, or if it's a fight they're looking for, competitive sports channel energy.

C Unruliness is merely a precursor to bravery! As long as they aren't hurting anyone, that is.

2 HOW WOULD YOU INTERACT WITH MEMBERS OF ANOTHER GELFLING CLAN?

A Peaceably and ceremoniously.

B With respect that is commensurate with the respect they offer me.

C Interact? I'd rather not.

3 WHEN FACED WITH A THREAT TO YOUR CLAN, HOW WOULD YOU REACT?

A I would attempt to negotiate, and prioritize the Gelfling who are counting on me. I always put my clan first.

B I would rally my clan, and encourage them to join me as we resist whatever threatens us—together.

C I would gather my clan, and focus on strategy and exercising our advantages, even if that means fleeing.

WOULD YOU RATHER?
SAIL THE SEA ON A
SIFAN SHIP, OR THE
CRYSTAL DESERT
ABOARD A DOUSAN
CRYSTAL SKIMMER?

4 WHAT CREATURE OF THRA ARE YOU MOST LIKE?

A   A Unamoth—transformative and beautiful.

B   A Fizzgig—scrappy and proud.

C   A Hollerbat—joyful and energetic.

5 HOW DO YOU REACT TO TRYING SOMETHING NEW?

A   In theory, I'm open to trying new things. However, finding the time to do so is not always possible.

B   I would jump in with both feet, so long as I know the stakes.

C   I'm sometimes reluctant to try new things. But I also know new experiences keep the mind fresh and agile, so I'll usually end up trying anyway.

6 HOW WOULD YOU PREFER TO RAISE YOUR CHILDREN?

A   With love and dedication.

B   With encouragement and discipline.

C   With a sense of humor and an open mind.

7 HOW WOULD OTHERS DESCRIBE YOU?

A   Orderly, intelligent, and compassionate.

B   Strong, willful, and bold.

C   Kind, friendly, and mischievous.

IF YOU ANSWERED MOSTLY A's, YOUR STYLE IS MOST LIKE MAUDRA MAYRIN'S!

Maudra Mayrin, also known as All-Maudra Mayrin, is the most recent in a long line of Vapran maudras. Chosen by the Skeksis long ago as the ambassador of the Gelfling clans, the All-Maudra has a special responsibility to represent not only her own clan, but the other six as well. For this reason, All-Maudra Mayrin often relies on decorum and precedent when making important decisions. Overall, Mayrin's style is objective and just; however, like any Gelfling might, she can still occasionally be seduced by the trappings of being the Skeksis' favored maudra . . .

IF YOU ANSWERED MOSTLY B's, YOUR STYLE IS MOST LIKE MAUDRA FARA'S!

Maudra Fara of the Stonewood clan is one of the most well-respected maudras of the current age. Many would say she earned her reputation thanks to the proximity her clan has to the Skeksis' castle—over the many trine that Maudra Fara has led the Stonewood, she has never angered or submitted to the Skeksis with whom she shares the Endless Forest and its surrounding regions. When it comes to discipline, Maudra Fara is the type to take matters into her own hands. Thanks to her do-it-yourself attitude, she has earned the undying respect of every Gelfling in her clan. They would all gladly go into battle with her, knowing she would be leading from the front lines.

IF YOU ANSWERED MOSTLY C's, YOUR STYLE IS MOST LIKE MAUDRA ARGOT'S!

Maudra Argot of the Grottan clan is the oldest living maudra. Both she and her clan benefit from her many trine of life experience, during which she has lived both within the Caves of Grot and outside of them. In her long life, she has learned two things: one, a sense of humor is the best way to stay young; and two, timing is everything. Maudra Argot is strategic and intelligent, but it is her optimism and ability to find the good in things that truly make her a strong leader. Still, even she can suffer from the disadvantages of old age; luckily she has many youngsters to keep her worldview evolving.

WHAT KIND OF GELFLING MAGIC DO YOU HAVE?

Gelfling magic is a special way that the Gelfling connect with Thra and the Crystal of Truth. But magic isn't limited to Gelfling. Perhaps your talents and gifts are just as magical—take this quiz to find out which kind of Gelfling magic you already have!

1 WHICH OF THESE CAREERS BEST SUITS YOU?

A   Therapist, mediator, or counselor
B   Meteorologist, salesperson, or travel guide
C   Writer, actor, or politician
D   Doctor, firefighter, or teacher

2 WHAT DO YOU CONSIDER YOUR GREATEST TALENT?

A   My ability to connect with others
B   My ability to read the emotions of others
C   My ability to explain things to others
D   My ability to comfort others

3 WHAT DO YOU CONSIDER YOUR GREATEST SHORTCOMING?

A   Sometimes I share too much about myself and expect others to do the same.
B   Sometimes I get anxious.
C   Sometimes I get lost in stories and forget reality.
D   Sometimes I forget to take care of myself.

4 IF YOU WENT ON A TRIP AND COULD ONLY BRING ONE BOOK, WHAT KIND OF BOOK WOULD IT BE?

A   An inspiring memoir
B   An encyclopedia of symbols
C   A dense fantasy novel
D   A cookbook with new recipes

5 WHEN A FRIEND IS HAVING A DIFFICULT TIME, HOW DO YOU SHOW YOUR SUPPORT?

A   I try to empathize with what they're going through.

B   I try to help them consider the meaning of their experience.

C   I tell them a story about a similar situation and how it turned out all right.

D   I try to find holistic remedies to reduce their suffering.

6 IF YOU COULD HAVE A SUPERPOWER, WHAT WOULD YOU CHOOSE?

A   The ability to communicate without words

B   Supernatural foresight

C   A perfect memory

D   The ability to sense and soothe pain

7 IF A FRIEND CONFESSED TO YOU THAT THEY HAD LIED ABOUT SOMETHING, HOW WOULD YOU REACT?

A   I would try my best to understand where they were coming from.

B   I already had a feeling, so I wouldn't be surprised. It's more important that they told me.

C   I would ask them to remember how they felt when they lied, in the hope that they wouldn't do it again in the future.

D   I would forgive them and encourage them to trust me.

8 WHAT QUALITY DO YOU THINK IS MOST IMPORTANT WHEN MAKING A POSITIVE DIFFERENCE IN THE WORLD?

A   Compassion—understanding that we are all connected

B   Foresight—looking toward a better future

C   Hindsight—learning from the stories of the past

D   Cultivation—nurturing the good in others

WOULD YOU RATHER? MEET AUGHRA OR THE EMPEROR SKEKSO?

ANSWER KEY

IF YOU ANSWERED MOSTLY A's, YOU ARE A DREAMFASTER!

Dreamfasting is the ability to psychically connect one-on-one with others, and requires great sensitivity, trust, and trustworthiness. Those that have the ability to dreamfast are able to see into the minds of others, and in turn are able to share their own feelings and experiences in a way that transcends words.

IF YOU ANSWERED MOSTLY B's, YOU ARE A FAR-DREAMER!

Far-dreaming is the ability to see into the future, both by interpreting the images in dreams and by listening to the messages whispered by the Crystal of Truth. Those with the ability to far-dream often have vivid dreams, or see signs where others see nothing. Far-dreamers also have the ability to "read" others, allowing them to predict what that person may do.

IF YOU ANSWERED MOSTLY C's, YOU ARE A DREAM-STITCHER!

Dream-stitching is the ability to fasten a memory to a physical object, which can then be passed on to others. Combining the skills of dreamfasting and dream-etching, dream-stitchers are able to tell powerful stories that invoke all the senses and stir the imagination. The stories can be transferred to others in a physical form, such as a book or painting.

IF YOU ANSWERED MOSTLY D's, YOU ARE A HEALER!

Gelfling healing magic is perhaps one of the most miraculous abilities of all. Healers are able to mend wounds, both physical and mental, by channeling the immense energy of Thra and the Crystal. One must be compassionate and loving in order to harness such powerful energy; healers are both, prioritizing the well-being of others above all else.